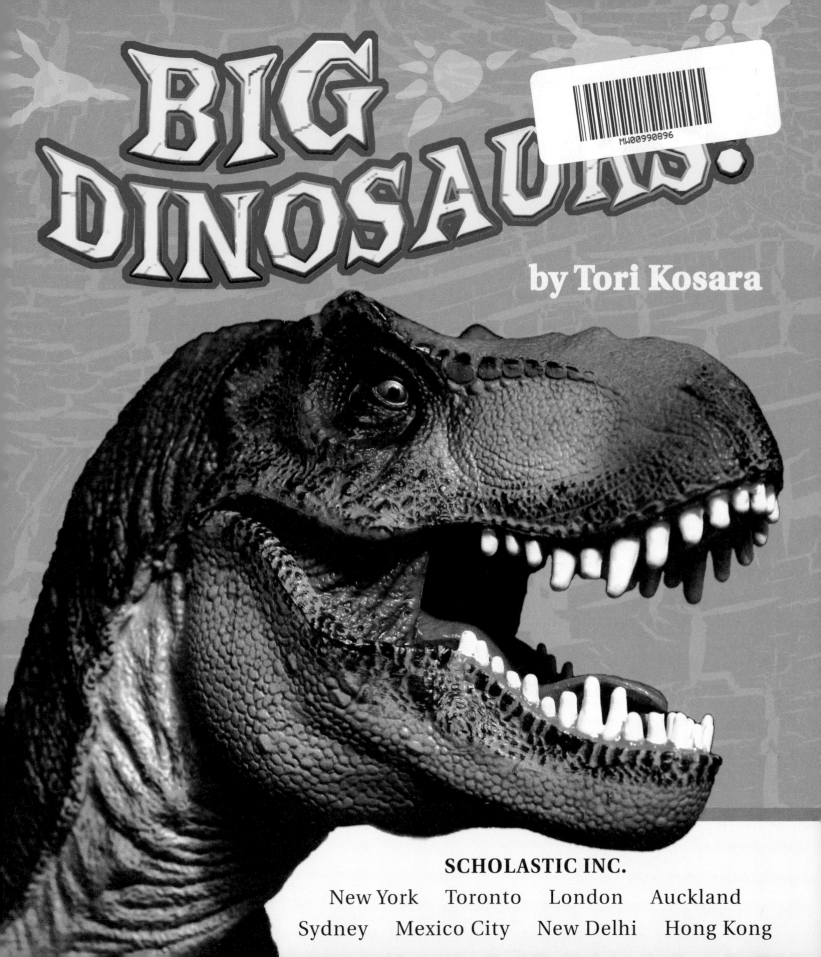

BIG DINOSAURS!

by Tori Kosara

SCHOLASTIC INC.

New York   Toronto   London   Auckland

Sydney   Mexico City   New Delhi   Hong Kong

Published by Scholastic Inc., *Publishers since 1920.*
SCHOLASTIC and associated logos are trademarks and/or registered trademarks of
Scholastic Inc.

ISBN 978-0-545-37956-4

10 9 8 7 6 5 4 3 2   11 12 13 14 15

Printed in the U.S.A.   40
First edition, September 2011

Designed by Charice Silverman

Front cover and title page: Kickers/Shutterstock; page 3: Photobank.Kiev.Ua/Shutterstock; pages
4–5: Christian Darkin/Photo Researchers; page 6: Paul Fleet/Shutterstock; page 7: Andreas Meyer/
Shutterstock; pages 8–9: Joe Tucciarone/Photo Researchers; pages 10–11: De Agostini/Gettyimages;
pages 12–13: Roger Harris/Photo Researchers; page 14: Linda Bucklin/Shutterstock; page 15: S_oleg/
Shutterstock; pages 16–17: Kenneth W Fink/Photo Reserchers; pages 18–19: Jason Lindsey/Alamy; page
19: Francois Gohier/Photo Researchers; pages 20–21: Roger Harris/Photo Researchers; page 22: Walter
Geiersperger/Corbis; pages 22–23: Joe Tucciarone/Photo Researchers; page 24: Kim Taylor/Warren
Photographers/Photo Researchers; page 25: Deagostino Editorial/Gettyimages; page 26: Francois
Gohier/Photo Researchers; pages 26–27: Jean Michel Girard/Shutterstock; pages 28–29: Roger Harris/
Photo Researchers; page 30: Take 27 Ltd/Photo Researchers; page 31: Wang Shuhai–Imaginechina/
Associated Press; back cover: Shutterstock

Dinosaurs were **reptiles** that first appeared on Earth around 230 million years ago! Humans did not live at the same time as dinosaurs, but scientists have discovered that there were once at least 500 different **species** of dinosaur.

How many types of dinosaur can you name?

Like most other reptiles, many female dinosaurs laid eggs in nests. Baby dinosaurs hatched from these eggs.

What other animals lay eggs?

ammonites

Birds and water animals that lived during the time of the dinosaurs are not called dinosaurs. Dinosaurs were **terrestrial**, or land-dwelling, animals.

elasmosaurus

What animals do you know that live only on land?

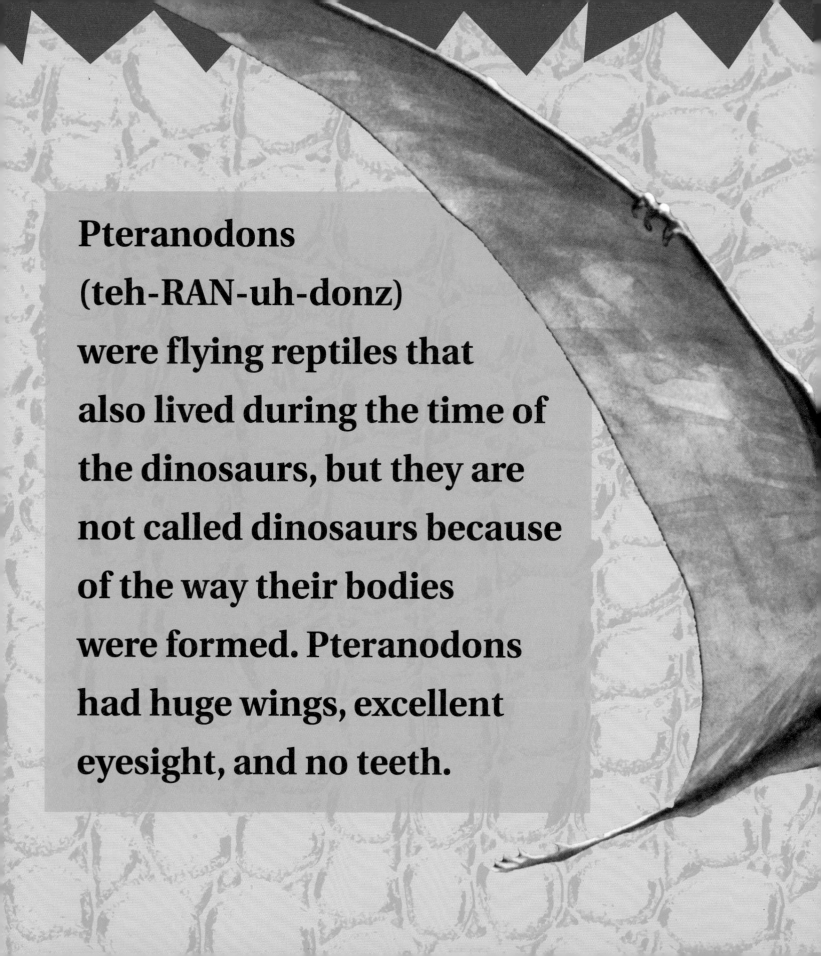

Pteranodons
(teh-RAN-uh-donz)
were flying reptiles that
also lived during the time of
the dinosaurs, but they are
not called dinosaurs because
of the way their bodies
were formed. Pteranodons
had huge wings, excellent
eyesight, and no teeth.

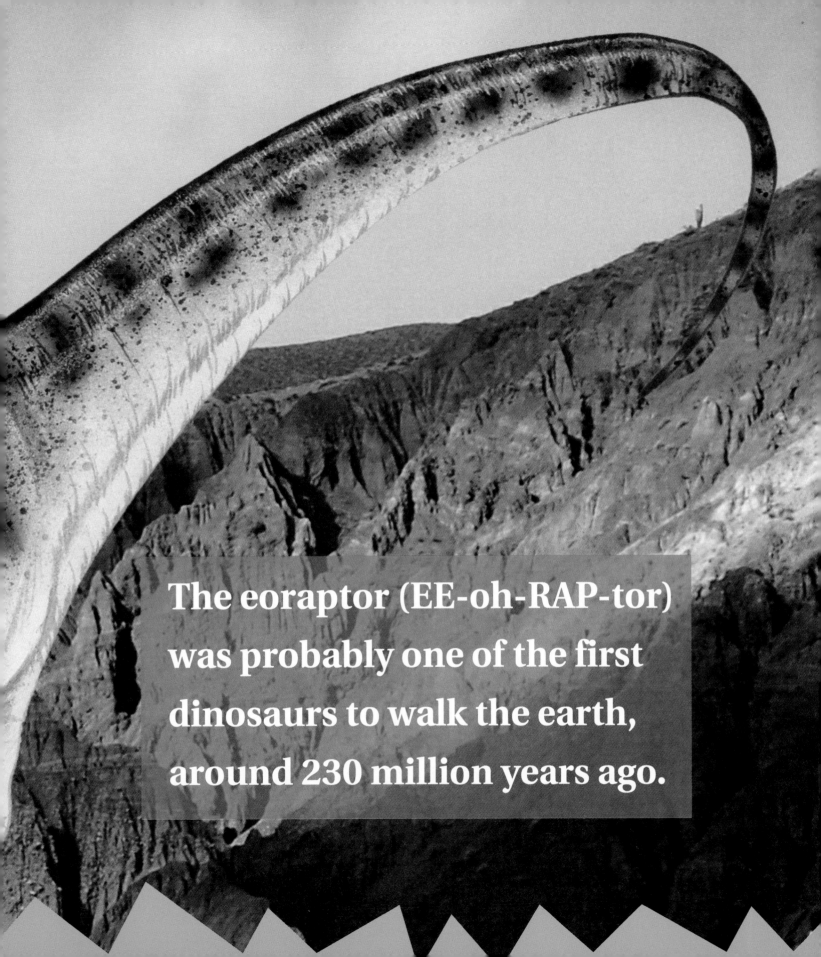

The eoraptor (EE-oh-RAP-tor) was probably one of the first dinosaurs to walk the earth, around 230 million years ago.

Dinosaurs were many different sizes. One of the tallest dinosaurs scientists have discovered is the brachiosaurus (BRAH-kee-oh-SORE-us). It was 75 feet long and 40 feet tall!

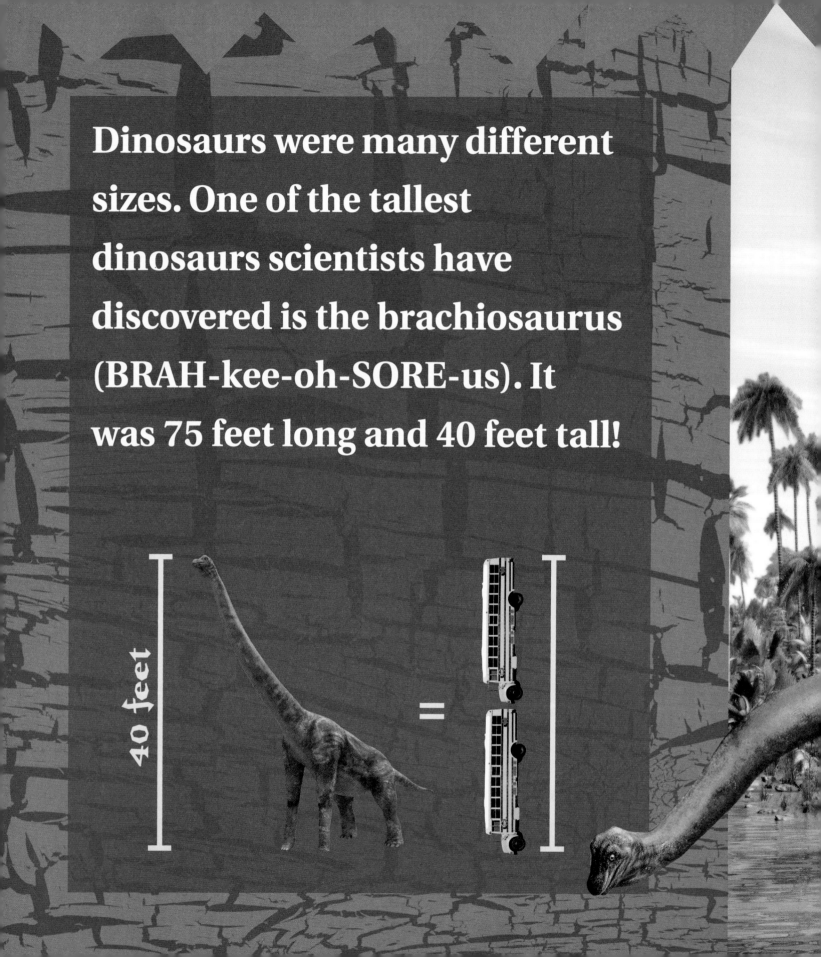

40 feet

=

One of the smallest dinosaurs scientists know of is the compsognathus (comp-sog-NAY-thus).

2.5 feet

A little larger than a
chicken, this tiny dinosaur
was just 2.5 feet tall.

Some dinosaurs were **carnivores**. They ate only meat. Many were **herbivores**, meaning they ate only plants.

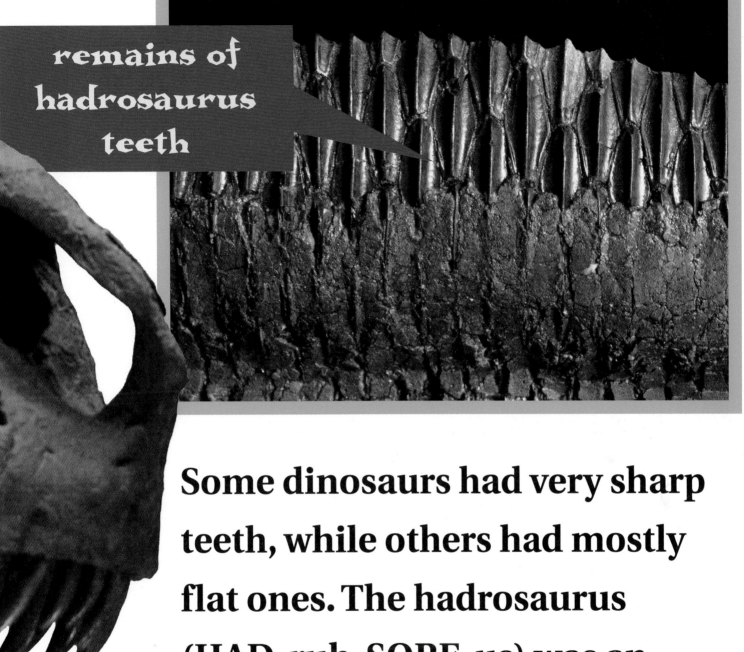

remains of hadrosaurus teeth

Some dinosaurs had very sharp teeth, while others had mostly flat ones. The hadrosaurus (HAD-ruh-SORE-us) was an herbivore. It could have about 250 flat teeth in its mouth at one time!

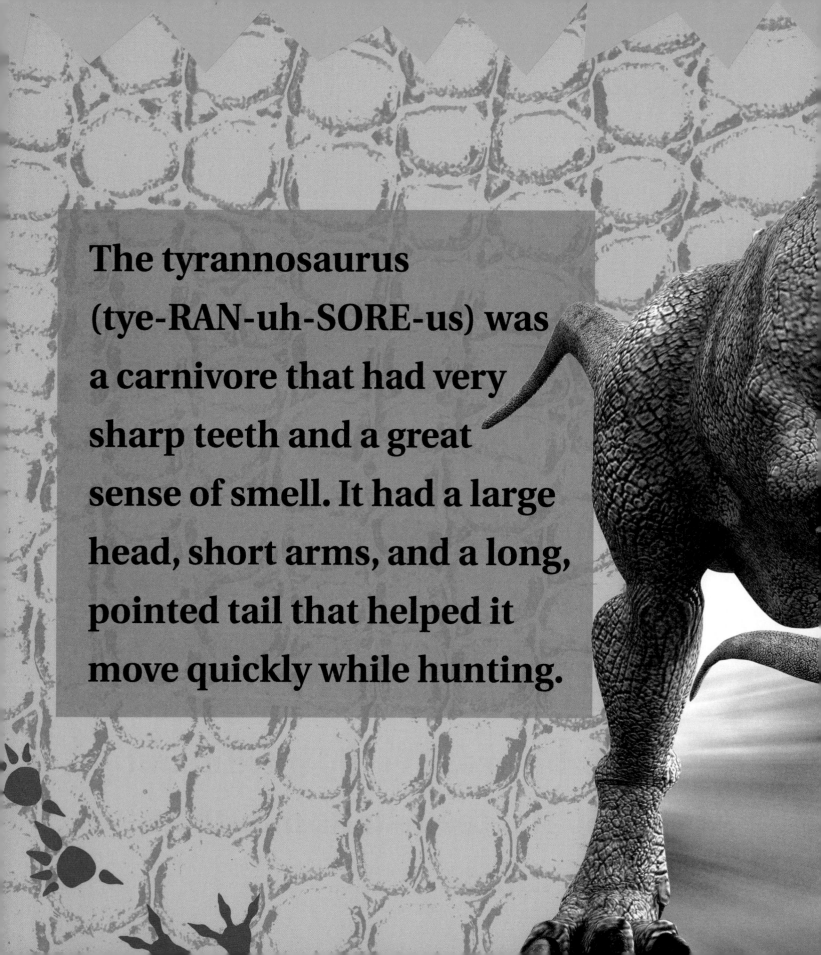

The tyrannosaurus (tye-RAN-uh-SORE-us) was a carnivore that had very sharp teeth and a great sense of smell. It had a large head, short arms, and a long, pointed tail that helped it move quickly while hunting.

close-up of claw

The velociraptor (veh-LAH-sih-RAP-tor) was an excellent hunter. Velociraptors used their long claws to help them catch food.

Scientists think that the smartest dinosaur may have been the troodon (TRO-uh-don), because it had an unusually large brain for a small dinosaur.

Most dinosaurs had scaly, bumpy skin. The stegosaurus (STEH-guh-SORE-us) had a row of plates down its back and spikes on its tail.

close-up of scales

Can you name any other animals that have scaly skin?

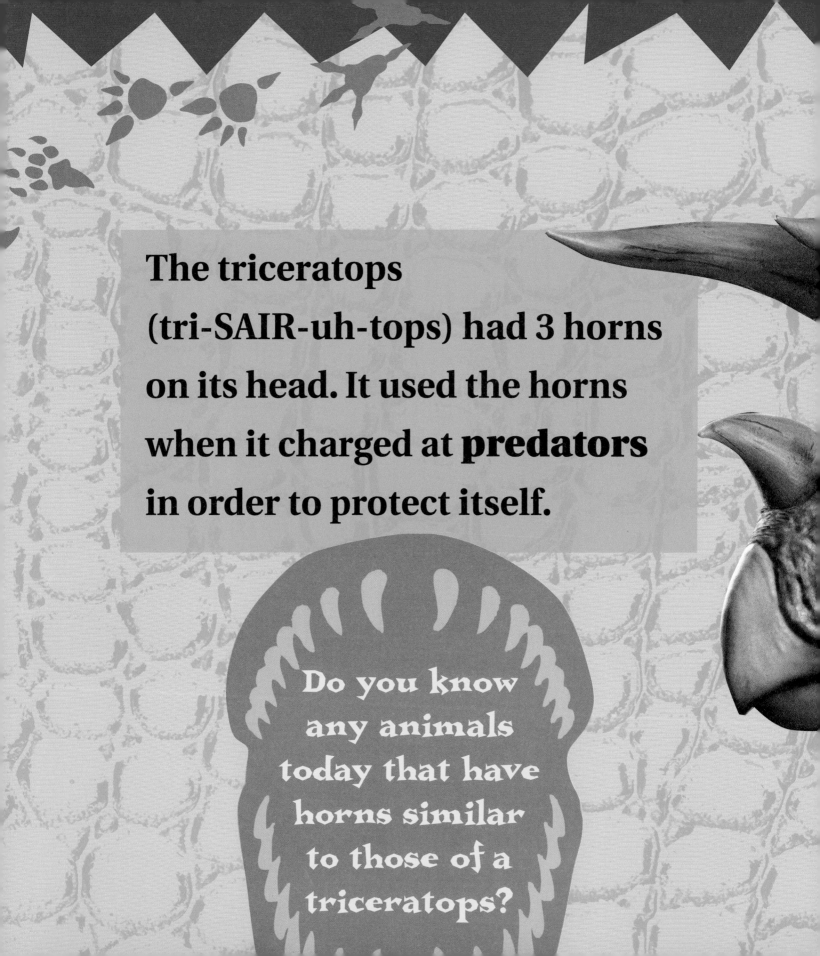

The triceratops (tri-SAIR-uh-tops) had 3 horns on its head. It used the horns when it charged at **predators** in order to protect itself.

Do you know any animals today that have horns similar to those of a triceratops?

Dinosaurs walked the earth for about 160 million years. No one knows what caused dinosaurs to become **extinct**. Scientists have many theories, or ideas. Some think that a large asteroid hit the earth and caused all the dinosaurs to die.

What do you think might have caused the dinosaurs to die out?

dinosaur footprints

Today, **fossils** are all that's left of the dinosaurs. Dinosaur fossils, such as bones, teeth, and footprints, have been found all over the world.

Glossary

Carnivore (KAR-nih-vor): An animal that eats meat.

Extinct (ek-STINKT): No longer existing.

Fossil (FAH-sul): A remnant or impression of an ancient plant or animal.

Herbivore (UR-bih-vor): An animal that eats plants.

Predator (PREH-duh-tor): An animal that hunts other animals for food.

Reptile (REP-tile): A cold-blooded animal.

Species (SPEE-seez): A class of things that have the same characteristics and the same name.

Terrestrial (teh-REHS-tree-uhl): Living on land.